Published by Creative Education
123 South Broad Street, Mankato, Minnesota 56001
Creative Education is an imprint of The Creative Company

Design and production by Stephanie Blumenthal
Printed in the United States of America

Photographs by Getty Images (Terje Rakke), Galyn C. Hammond, JLM Visuals (Burton A. Amundson, Charlie Crangle,
Robert Greenler, Ken & Helga Heiman, Richard P. Jacobs, Breck P. Kent, John Minnich, Mike Reblin), Robert McCaw,
Eugene G. Schulz, Tom Stack & Associates (Terry Donnelly, Jeff Foott, Sharon Gerig, Barbara Gerlach, Thomas Kitchin,
Joe McDonald, Allen B. Smith, Doug Sokell, Spencer Swanger), Unicorn Stock Photos (Robert E. Barber)

Library of Congress Cataloging-in-Publication Data

Bodden, Valerie.
Glaciers / by Valerie Bodden.
p. cm. — (Our world)
Includes index.
ISBN-13 : 978-1-58341-462-0
1. Glaciers—Juvenile literature. I. Title. II. Series.
GB2403.8.B63 2006   551.31'2—dc22   2005053721

First Edition
2 4 6 8 9 7 5 3 1

OUR WORLD

G L A C I E R S

Valerie Bodden

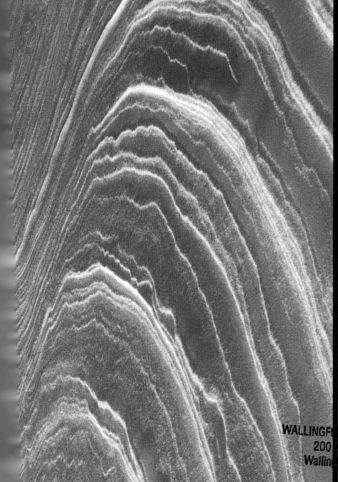

Glaciers (GLAY-shurs) are huge pieces of ice. They cover big areas of land. Glaciers are found in cold parts of the world. Most glaciers are on **mountains**. Some of the biggest glaciers are at the North Pole. There are glaciers at the South Pole, too.

Not all glaciers look the same. Some glaciers look white. Others look blue! Some glaciers look smooth. Other glaciers look cracked.

Every glacier looks a little different

Glaciers do not stay still. They slide over the ground very slowly. Many glaciers slide down the sides of mountains! Some glaciers slide about 300 feet (91 m) a year. That is as long as a football field. Other glaciers slide 10 times faster.

Glaciers slide to the bottom of mountains

When glaciers slide, they run over things. Some glaciers run over trees. Some of the trees are big. But glaciers are strong. They knock the trees down!

Glaciers have a lot of pushing power

Glaciers run over rocks, too. Some of the rocks are small. But others are big **boulders**. The boulders can be bigger than a house! Lots of rocks and boulders get stuck in glaciers. The glaciers push them to the bottom of the mountain.

Glaciers run over lots of dirt. The dirt makes glaciers look brown in some places. It makes the ice look dirty!

Glaciers pick up dirt from the ground

Some glaciers keep moving until they reach the **sea**. They hang over the water. Then big pieces of  ice break off of the glaciers. The ice falls into the water. It makes a big splash! The pieces of ice that fall in the water are called icebergs.

In some places, the sea is full of icebergs

Glaciers help make icebergs and waterfalls

Sometimes it gets warm out. Then glaciers start to **melt**. Water runs off of the glaciers. Some of the water runs into streams. Some of the water forms pretty waterfalls!

People can visit some glaciers. They can fly airplanes over the glaciers. They can take pictures of the glaciers. Sometimes they can even walk on the glaciers!

Most glaciers are much taller than people

Glaciers pick up rocks and dirt. You can make your own dirty glacier. Fill a plastic bag half full of water. Put a handful of dirt in the bag. Add a few rocks. Tie the bag shut. Put it in the freezer. Take it out after a few days. What does your glacier look like?

GLOSSARY

boulders—very big rocks

melt—when ice turns into water

mountains—very big hills

sea—a very big area of water that has salt in it

LEARN MORE ABOUT GLACIERS

Glacier Bay
http://www.isset.org/site_of_
the_month/glacier_bay/
images.html

Glacier Jigsaw Puzzle
http://www.surfnetkids.com/
games/glacier-js.htm

Classroom Clipart: Glaciers
http://classroomclipart.com/
cgi–bin/kids/imageFolio.cgi?
direct=Geography/Glaciers